Inside Her Mind

Subha

BookLeaf
Publishing

India | USA | UK

Presentation by *BookLeaf Publishing*

Web: www.bookleafpub.com

E-mail: info@bookleafpub.com

ISBN: 9789363307957

First edition 2024

Fragments of Me

You are strong,
You are beautiful,
You are brave,
they say.
But why won't they notice,
I'm breaking day by day.
Rain's a camouflage of the tears
in my face,
Hidden from your view
in a cage I made.
Do I deserve to live?
or do I deserve to die?
Like shattered glass,
I'm broken inside.

Echoes of a Shattered Soul

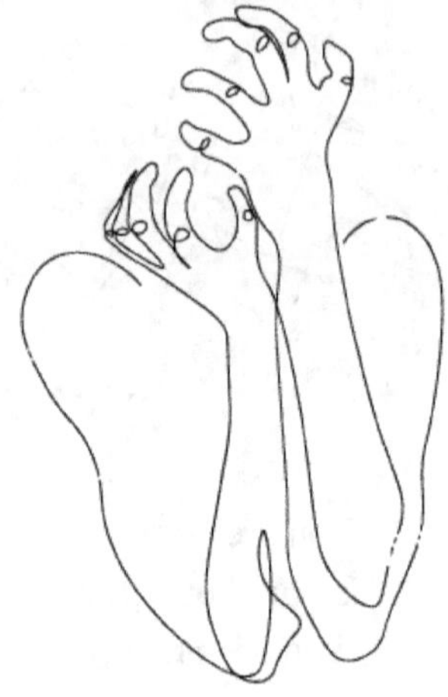

The weight of the world bears down on me.
A million voices whispering,
no one really knows me.
They simply just... don't.
They see what I show,
They dig if they care.
But I don't know my way,
the roads all collide.
Lost within myself,
blinded in my own maze.
A hidden force in a sea of lies
buried in the crevices,
of space and time.
Impossible to ever reach

I grow tall,
from my tears,
from broken glass and burned coal.
I grow with my mask held high.
A sea of red drips from my back,
From the holes
where the knives inside me,
are carved and frozen in stone.

The Price of Peace

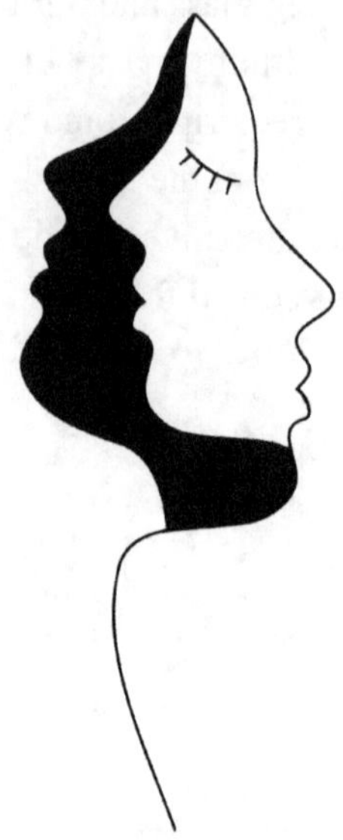

Hearts Break,
like glass.
Trust,
a thing of the past.
We sit and wait,
watching ourselves die inside.
We can't fight,
so we hide.
From the pain, the past,
the blood smeared under the mask.
I'm not to blame,

but I suffer regardless.
My mouth sewn shut,
my voice erased,
I give you everything.
Blindly, Defeated,
So
Lose my peace
And
Lose my life

Echoes of the Tempest

Rich Ambrosia
Dive Of Pleasure
Tempestuous Sire
Call Of The Lost
Distant And Cold
Away Yet Never So Close
The Waves Of Pain Wash Away
I Just Can't Everyday

The Edge of Desire

In front of me,
yet we can't connect.
Lost in your eyes.
drowning.
Passion pulling me close,
yet still so far.
Never knew love,
until it was torn apart.
Been hurt too much,
it's all a lie.
Near touch,
A breath too far
Near touch,
Falling apart.

Illusion of Love

What is love?
A word shrouded in shadows, tangled in beliefs,
It becomes what you perceive it to be.

Love was a crazed fantasy where you believed
"we were meant to be"
Those nostalgic, bittersweet childhood
memories.
Eyes fall upon your beloved,
        and your world changes ever so slightly.
Was that love or just a silly dream?
I can't recall, It's ancient history.

Was it love with my mind at war?
        their touch, their smell, their taste
It seems to haunt me.

The memory lingers past its time,
        despite its thorns,
it was mine.

Was it love after all the pain?
Maybe it was. Maybe for me.
Or maybe it just wasn't meant to be.

My pain, My solace
Was it a wound that bleeds,
        was it a wound that bleeds,
Or the balm that heals me?

I loved too early,
        I loved too fast,
I loved too late,
        I never learned to love.
I don't know but with time, we'll see.
Was it true love
        or a terrible fantasy?

Memory of You

The cold air kissed my skin,
yet it was your breath that entered my lungs,
keeping me warm and safe.
In our little bubble, we stood.
Your hands around the place my mind claimed
abode.
The hum of the cars, the birds, the chatter miles
away,
the sway of the leaves falling, ignored.
Winded down, often misplaced,
the glorious red hues we embraced.
And we stayed, and stayed, and stayed.
Your kiss failed to bring me back to life.

I was a flower, you my scythe.
I stood transfixed, I had a home,
even if only for a while.
I looked in your eyes, you were mine.
you were mine and I was yours,
even if only for a while.

Bleeding Scars

Time heals all wounds; that much is true.
Yet the scar you left bleeds every time I see you.
Why it pours, I'm not sure.
What's worse is you were my pain and my cure.
I worshiped the land you walked on,
Didn't expect you to pull me underneath.
Like a magnet, I was hypnotized, quite simply.
Pulled closer and closer till I could no more.
Why draw me in just to let me go?
You broke my walls just to build another,
Why, you were my only pain, lover.

The Weight of Regret

I'm sorry my words break glass.
I'm sorry my trust couldn't be given so fast.
My life intertwined with yours,
I'm sorry my heart is made of brass.
I try and try,
     but my hands slip past,
  like sand, like sea
I just couldn't move past.
It hurt to see you go,
     but I could not be your home.
You needed peace, you needed safety…
     safety, security,
  I could never be that.
My mind a tsunami, chaos ensured a guarantee.
I could not give, what was once taken from me.
I'm sorry.

In the Ashes of Love

Your words were lies,
your eyes a dream.
You promised I could fall,
but you never did catch me.
Promises, Poison, it all happened so fast,
crashed and burned,
we were supposed to last.
You didn't think twice,
before you made your choice.
Was I an option, or simply second choice?
You chose pain, You chose tears.
You chose history.
Why, when I offered you every victory?
I guess you liked the pain,

fooled yourself into believing things would
change.
You never learned,
you had to make your own mistakes.
I would've stayed. I would've stayed,
but you didn't stay long enough to find out that
was the case.
Promises, Poison, it all happened so fast.
We Crashed, We Burned.
I deserved better than that.

Her Name

Words of honey,
silky and smooth.
Flew so high,
until you stuck me with a noose.
It passed your lips,
sharp and raw.
Split my heart in half,
exposing a wound I thought was small.
The world went blank,
silent, and still.
My heart dropped,
shrinking within.
"It was a mistake." Let's say I believe.
Were we?
Were we or were you just used to
her harmony?

Essence of Us

Our souls bound,
grounded in fantasy.
So far gone,
even the fates would weep.
Intertwined threads,
sealed with an unspoken plea.
Every single touch pulled me deep.
We reached highs,
beyond compare.
My dignity,
simply stripped bare.
Nothing but pure ecstasy,
every breath I took was bound to your heartbeat.
Who do I turn to?
If my essence ran through your veins.
Losing you felt like losing a part of me.

Whispers of the Night

My heart heavy,
    does nothing but call your name.
Forgetting everything with the dying sun,
    on a bed of bloom, I lay.
The promise of peace dances around me,
    yet I feel compelled to slip into the dark.
Ten Minutes? Hours? Days?
    How long till I'm one with it?
Under the starry night, it all seems to fade away.
    How long can I truly stay?

The Lament of the Wayward Soul

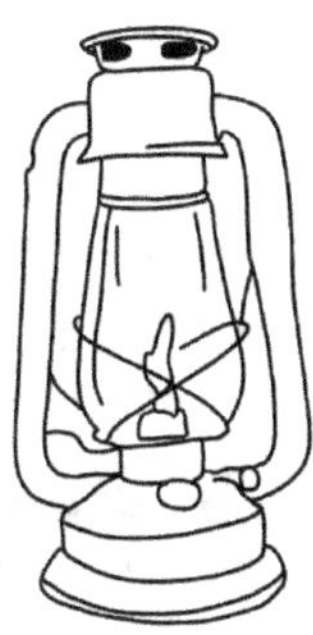

Is this a new page,
or a road I have already gauged?
Am I walking down paths,
with roads unscathed?
Tell me which way to go.
I do not know.
I do not know.
With my peace burned,
Who do I call home?

The Curse of Memory

Days pass as I stay here.
Grounded in place, frozen in time,
perfectly preserved.
The days turn into nights,
the nights into days.
My heart screams,
yet my mind doesn't seem to embrace.
The hues become a blur,
some timeless few.
My mind wants to forget,
yet all it does is remember you.

In the Wake of You

Words flow freely,
my hands bound.
My mind collides,
with you around.
My peace, my sanity,
seemingly blending into one.
Can't you tell?
I can't stay until you're done.

The Price of Admiration

It's all the same,
It's all the same.
You built me up so high.
Because you loved to watch me fall.
It's all the same,
It's all the same.
You admired how I crumbled.
Your ego inflated.
Another one down.
My body defeated.
It's all the same,
It's all the same.
You loved when the river pooled in my eyes.
It meant I cared.
But my smile wasn't nearly as worthy.
If it was me who smiled.

Chasing Fading Dreams

I used to pray every day,
 that somehow my mind would be cleared
away.
Waiting for time to take its course,
 I begged for a miracle,
 for someone to take my place.
But nothing changed,
 and time moved ahead.
My pleas unheard,
 my dreams hung on a thread.
Walking through shadows, chasing passing light,
 haunted by whispers, lost in the cruel night.
Hope seemed distant and out of reach.
A fading memory,
 too faint to ever teach.

Journey Back Home

It seems quiet, It seems okay.
But when my mind wanders,
My heart sways.
Against the tide,
A force unknown.
Destroying everything I've ever known.
Tell me how, I can't do this alone.
I can't forget the thing,
that shadows my dawn.
I search for solace,
I try to hold on.
Yet the voices linger in dreams unknown.
A tale unraveled,
a truth not told.
Searching for land,
a way back home.

In the Wake of Goodbye

Our hearts once fused, a cruel fantasy.
My world shattered with words I couldn't
believe.
All things come to an end, yes indeed.
But I could never imagine it happening to me.

Time, persistent, had performed its duty.
For the bloom that celebrated us, had shriveled
up entirely.
Our hearts, once fused, now unsure.
Parting ways because I deserved more.

Your words in mind, body, and soul.
I carry with me all I need.
With a heavy heart, I know to be true.
In the depths of sorrow, I learn to be whole.
For once I loved, I could once more.
Finding the strength to finally let go.

Heart of a Survivor

Your face bears the scars,
I can see it in your eyes.
I'm sure it was rough to hold on to your last
breath,
One can only take so much.
It wasn't a cure,
yet you made sure,
You had way more.
In mind and spirit,
stayed and held your own hand.
And, love, you were your own sun.
That's all you'll ever need.